Ithamer

and

Other Poems

Ithamer

and

Other Poems

by Sharon Hunt

With a contribution by Brooke Ouzts
Edited by V. Brice Hunt

Shoal Creek, L.C.

Enoch, UT

ISBN 978-0-615-94495-1

*In loving memory of
Sharon Hunt.*

Table of Contents

Editor's Preface

All but one or two of the poems in this book were written by my mother, Sharon Hunt. The poem, "Grandma Sharon's Last Poem," was written by one of Sharon's granddaughters, Brooke Ouzts. Another poem included is of unknown origin. "Christmas," found on page 25, was among my mother's papers without any indication of who wrote it. A search online turned up no hints about its origin nor was I able to find it in any other work or anthology; therefore, I believe that "Christmas" was likely written by either my mother or somebody that she personally knew. With those two exceptions, the poems in this book are definitively known to be written by my mother, Sharon Hunt.

Much of my mother's poetry tells stories. Many of the stories are true and are about her family or her ancestors. "Ithamer of the Big Feet," "The Freighter," and "The Colt" are examples of poems that tell true stories about real people. Other poems tell a fictional story, such as "The Lost Crown" or "Doby Plays Hookey."

Sharon's feelings about various situations were another major inspiration for her poems. Poems such as "Pinenut Picking Time," "The Dentist," or "My Husband Is a Cowboy" tell how she felt about various situations and common events in her life. Her love poems tell how she felt about her husband and family.

A few poems were written just for fun, such as "The Huggasaurus" and "Edjacation." A few other poems were written for a specific purpose. For example, "The Iverson Family Song" was written for a family reunion and "More Than Just a Mark" was written for an LDS Relief Society lesson.

While almost all of her poems conveyed some sort of moral to be learned, some of them were explicitly about the moral, such as "The Lord's Sabbath" and "Gossip."

All in all, the poetry in this book conveys the sentimentality and love that my mother had for God, for family, and for life.

V. Brice Hunt, Editor
January, 2014

The Huggasaurus

To Cody and Sharon

The Huggasaurus gives a hug,
To everything he sees—
So don't expect to get away,
Until you've had a squeeze—

The Tickedactyl tickles you,
Until you screech with laughter,
Prepare for lots of grins,
If you're the one he's after.

Then finally, there's the Shynosaur,
Who's just worked up the nerve,
To send you lots and lots of love,
The kind that you deserve.

Ithamer of the Big Feet

Let me tell you the story of Ithamer,
A youth both strong and tall,
Who ran chasing his father's oxen,
down a long and muddy draw.

>As he ran, his large feet sliding,
>In the boggy slippery clay,
>Leaving elongated footprints,
>As though a giant had passed that way.

Soon a fellow townsman came hunting,
His cattle had gone astray,
When he saw those over-sized footprints,
He was frightened and ran away.

>"O' men of the town come quickly!"
>He shouted out long and loud,
>Come see what I have discovered,
>And to the footprints he lead that crowd.

An alarm went over the settlement,
The people in total dismay,
All but Ithamer and his friend, Hans Peter,
Who chuckled and sauntered away.

>This gave the pair an idea,
>"Why not keep it going," they said,
>"A practical joke won't harm the folks,
>A good laugh we'll enjoy instead."

From boards they fashioned giant footprints,
Leather straps were fashioned on tight,
Then Ithamer would wear these wooden shoes
And walk about at night.

With each following day new prints were found,
In, about and around the town,
Men with guns would guard the way,
To keep families safe for work and play.

The night of the dance in the community,
Ithamer thought, "What a great opportunity,
To cause a ſtir and make them sweat,
This would be the beſt chance yet!"

Standing on ſtilts very tall,
And wearing a mask he watched the ball,
Looking through a window of the school,
When horrified dancers spied the ghoul.

Women screamed and children cried,
Men rushed for guns and ran outside,
Around the school with arms they swarmed,
If they found that giant they'd do him harm!

But he was gone! They began a search,
Around the school and beyond the church.
Then in the bushes they heard a sound,
They cocked their guns and crept around.

Then from the brush ſtepped a small spotted calf,
All Ithamer could do was ſtep aside and laugh.
"Friend," Hans Peter said, "I think we better tell,
They are so frightened that things may not turn out well."

When they told their ſtory,
Town folks were pretty riled,
Their attitudes about the joke
were anything but mild.

The Cave

While hiking the hills of Old Mexico,
Two young explorers just happened to go
To the side of a hill where they chanced to find
The long deserted shaft of a mine.

With a pine pitch torch to use as a light,
They decided to enter that cave, black as night,
They had to stoop as they entered in,
The entrance was no higher than either boy's chin.

They followed the cave as it turned and it twisted,
Their curious nature could not be resisted,
The going was rough, sometimes at a crawl,
Watching their steps to keep from a fall.

Back into the hill the cavern had wandered,
Upon reaching the end much time had been squandered.
When they finally arrived what they found was most shocking,
Their hearts started pointing and their knees went to knocking.

For curled together in a little fur ball,
All nestled up napping near to the wall,
Three little bear cubs peered up at the light,
They whined and they whimpered as the boys stared in fright.

Quickly they scrambled to get out of that place,
They feared they would meet mother bear face to face!
As in a vision they could plainly visualize
Hideous claws and fangs ending their lives.

Their torch was extinguished in their haste to depart,
Leaving the cave blacker than an evil man's heart.
Blacker than ink or blacker than soot,
Feeling their way out with hand and with foot.

In their terror and flurry, they bumped head and face,
Gouged shins and knees and hands in the race,
Trying to get out of that black confinement before
The mother bear decided to come in the door.

They were bloody and battered when they finally came out,
The first thing they did was start looking about.
It was then that they noticed that old mother bear's track,
And those boys skedaddled and never looked back.

Mother Love

Little arms that hold so tight,
Rosy lips that say good night,
Precious child when I am sad
You smile at me and make me glad.

Sparkling eyes clear as the sky,
Little hands that wave bye, bye.
Ten tiny toes so pink and sweet,
A button nose and busy feet.

Darling child so full of glee,
God sent you to help teach me,
You came to me from up above
And filled my heart with Mother Love.

The New Birthday Dress

Back in olden days when granny was very young,
She only owned a dress or two, which were kept so neatly hung.
One of them she wore to school, one she saved for church,
The oldest one, faded and patched was for play and work.
Every night her mama dear, would hang her dress with care,
But if it was soiled, she washed it and hung it on a chair.

One year on her birthday, she woke early in the morn,
To find a beautiful new dress that her mama had lovingly sewn.
"Oh mama, can I put it on and wear it through the day?
I promise I won't soil it when I work and play!"
"Oh no! you must save it until party time is near,
You may get it soiled and have to wear your old one, dear."

Granny kept on pleading, "I will keep it clean you know!"
"OK," said her mother, "I have told you 'NO,' so—
If you get it dirty, to the party it will not go."
"Oh thank you mama, I promise I'll use the greatest care,
I'll keep it clean the whole day long. I love you mama dear."
And she went through the morning singing songs of cheer.

Back in those olden times, if you wanted chicken dinner
you had to chop off the chicken's head, and take out all its innards.
When her mama went to the chicken yard, where she would catch the hen,
Granny wanted to come along and see, she stood well away, but then—
That chicken, when she lost her head, went flopping all around—
She splashed granny's dress with blood, before falling on the ground.

Poor, poor granny, her lovely dress was soiled,
She could not wear it to the party now, her chance for that was spoiled.
"I'll have no crying or tantrums," her mama said, "for those I do not care,
Go change into your old dress and I'll help you fix your hair."
Granny learned a lesson that she remembered all her life,
Listen when your parents speak, and avoid a lot of strife.

Service

When we help a friend or neighbor,
When we serve with pure intent,
When we do what is sorely needed
The love we feel is heaven sent.

When we serve with acts of kindness,
When we go the second mile,
We will feel so good inside us,
For helping others through a trial.

If a brother is hungry or homeless,
Wandering lost through this cold land,
Offer him your help and friendship,
Give to him your helping hand.

If a child needs understanding
Listen carefully with your heart,
If a neighbor needs forgiveness,
Offer him a clean new start.

When we serve our fellow beings,
When we show respect and care,
When we have our own times of sorrow,
Love and helping hands are there.

Let us control our tongues and tempers,
Treating others all the while,
As we would like to be treated,
Serving others with a smile.

Modena (Part I)

The lonesome train whistle blowing,
Now as it did then,
Restless cattle bawling and milling about their pen,
Nostalgic sights and sounds return from days gone by,
Tugging at the heart strings
Can make a grown man cry!

The railroad was Modena's claim to fame.
Travelers through-out the West came to know its name.
Leaders of the LDS Church traveling through the state,
Met wagons here, and buggies, which for them had come to wait.
Then haul them on to Dixie land
Over hills and rocks and deep red sand.

O, Modena was not always as small as it is today,
It was often busy with travelers going on their way.
Huge herds of cattle to be shipped through-out the land,
Were often penned up in corrals,
Then loaded on the train.

B. J. Lund owned the general store
And also the hotel,
The hospitality that they offered folks
Was thought of very well.

Freighters hauling loads of freight
To other settlements through-out the state,
Hauling flour or barrels of brew,
Some of it went to Nevada, too.

This is where my real story begins,
My Grandpa Hunt was one of them.

The Freighter (Part II)

Pioche, Nevada, was a tough mining town
Around eighteen-ninety-eight,
Elias Hunt braved desert heat and snow,
As he hauled wagon loads of freight.

From Utah's whistle stop called Milford,
Or old Modena's loading docks,
He hauled the freight to Nevada's miners,
Over roads of dirt and rocks.

Elias was a strong man
Who never took a drink,
So when the freight was spirits,
It arrived full to the brink.

One day Elias walked into a barroom,
There to get his pay,
While waiting for his money,
Glanced around, 'twas the close of day.

An old Indian sat on a bar stool
Over a glass he hung his head,
His eyes were closed and he was so still,
You'd have thought that he was dead.

When in swaggered a young cowboy,
He chose to take a seat,
Next to the old Indian,
And he never missed a beat.

The cowpoke's hand reached out quickly,
In a flash he snatched the glass,
In seconds he had downed the contents,
Shoved it back in one quick pass.

The old Indian's eyes barely opened,
He peered at that cowboy with a frown,
"You thinkee you so smart,
    me drinkee three times and he no ſtay down!"

To this ſtory there is a moral,
It is there for young and old,
Do not think you are smarter,
Do not dare to be so bold!

Do not try to take advantage
Of the weak or of the poor,
Or you might be like that cowboy
who went rushing for the door!

Edjacation

Ain't edjacation woner'ful,
Fer them that goes ta school?
It takes em a lotta years ta learn
Ta be an edjacated fool!

Why I had an edjacation,
My pappy gave ta me,
He took me out behind the barn,
When I was only three!

I'll tell ya that I learned how
Ta slop them hogs jiſt swell,
Ta gather up them aigs,
N' draw water frum the well.

I ain't much on book learnin'
As you can plainly tell.
I'd write m'name but I forgot
How it's supposed ta spell!

The Dentist

When I go to the dentist
I am so forlorn
I'm always dejected
and also quite torn

I know I've gotta go there
but I wanta stay here
The song of the drill
might just bring on a tear!

And needles, oh my,
how they do offend!
What I need about now
Is a very good friend.

One who will go
to the dentist for me
Get my teeth filled
and return them for free!

There is one little hitch
That this plan is about
Even if she'd take um,
I can't get um out!

Swinging and Chewing

When Granny Leoma was very small,
She thought her life just had it ALL,
if—
She had a swing and a piece of gum.
Swinging and chewing was so much fun,
Chewing and swinging through the air
Was better than ribbons in her hair,
Was better than running,
and playing tag,
or swimming,
or climbing up high
Yes! When chewing and swinging
Up in the sky,
Swinging and chewing from the limb of a tree.
That was the way life ought to be!

A Young Man and His Cat

There was a young man
Who wore a high hat
And pranced around England
Along with his cat.

They went to the Palace
to visit the Queen
He stepped on her tail
and made the cat sing.

The Queen was annoyed,
And sent them away,
They went to Bermuda
And there they will stay.

Pinenut Picking Time

It's a fun and festive time of year
When Pinenut picking time is here.
We gather our buckets and our sacks,
And for Pinion country make our tracks.

Beneath the Pinion trees so tall,
Nuts, very tasty, brown and small,
Among the needles on the ground,
Like an apron spread around.

Inviting to both man and beast,
A pocket full will make a feast.
When roasting up the nuts just so,
It surely makes the juices flow.

Pine needles prick my hands and knees
As I kneel on the carpet beneath the trees,
Gathering nuts into my pail,
While breezes blow and soft clouds sail.

Weary muscles are glad for rest,
At end of day we've done our best.
Gathering bounty in Nature's ways,
To enjoy on frigid winter days.

Get on Your Pony

With Talia

Get on your horse and take a ride,
All around the countryside,
Ride him fast and ride him slow,
Getty up, Getty up, Go horse go!

Get on your pony and go for a run,
It will be a lot of fun,
Ride him up and ride him down,
Ride him all around the town.

My Mother's Face

When I was small as I could be
Sitting on my mother's knee,
She held me tight and smiled at me,
Time etched that face in memory.

When I began to venture forth
To do things on my own,
I'd seek her face and reassuring smile,
And I'd know that I wasn't alone.

A face so full of love and care,
To me is beauty beyond compare,
Though lined and chiseled from toil and pain,
Her gentle strength and faith are plain.

I look to her in all I do,
Her kindly face is honest and true,
Again, I hope to see her smile,
Content and happy all the while.

The Lord's Sabbath

The Sabbath is the Lord's day,
It's only one in seven,
Just one day to remember
the creator of earth and heaven.
He sacrificed His life for us,
He showed to us the way,
He loves us and forgives us
when e'er we go astray.

He waits for us with open arms,
He hears us when we pray,
Can we not take time for Him,
on His Holy day?
How can we selfishly forget
all the things He's done?
We trample Him beneath our feet
all in the name of fun!

The Sabbath day was set aside,
a time for thoughtfulness,
To remember and to worship Him,
and pray our lives to bless,
The Sabbath is the Lord's day,
only one day of the week,
Worship Him and keep His day,
and His presence seek.

Will we choose to follow Him
and live our lives in peace,
Will we show to Him our love
and honor Him each week?
He has given us our very lives,
allowed us to be free,
He is waiting there just to see
what we will choose to be.

My Husband Is a Cowboy

My husband is a cowboy,
He's been one all his life,
You can bet I've learned a lot
Since I became his wife!

I've learned about hard toil,
In snow, or driving rain,
Those old cows must be fed
Before he comes home again.

A cowboy's life is getting up
Early in the dawn,
Eating dust behind the herd
Until the sun is gone.

The old pick-up truck rattles and squeaks
Down a bumpy lane,
Carrying him to distant pasture or pond
And bringing him back again.

His life is not easy,
It takes a real man!
He's willing to give what it takes,
For he loves the life-style and the land!

The Colt

Your grandpa is a cowboy, he's been one all his days,
He worked from dawn to sundown, without much pay or praise.
Even at the age of three, day after day, with a carrot in his hand,
He coaxed a colt up by the fence, he was sure he could command.

One day he accomplished his desire, the colt approached to be fed,
He slipped the inner ring of a tire over the yearling's head,
With a rope tied firm to the ring and then to his little red wagon tongue,
Gramps climbed into the wagon and clucked, he was set for a lot of fun.

The colt set off at a canter right down the middle of the street,
Gramps felt like he had really done it, freedom oh so sweet!
Then something happened! The wheel came off old red.
A neighbor came shouting, "That colt will kick off the boy's head!"

But gramps ran to the prancing colt, after climbing out of old red.
"Whoa! Whoa!" He soothed the animal, and the colt lowered his head.
Gramp's mother came running out of the house in distress,
Only to find all the excitement was not a worrisome mess.

Gramp's daddy just chuckled, and patted gramps on the head,
From then on he said the colt was broken,
It handled and led smooth as sand.
Broke by love and carrot, and the touch of a little boy's hand.

When I Pray

To Sharon

I love my Heavenly Father,
I pray to Him each day,
I thank Him for watching over me
When I work and play.

I know Heavenly Father loves me,
and when I kneel and pray
I'll never be left all alone,
not even for a day.

I have no need to be afraid
Just kneel down and pray
and Heavenly Father will protect me
Each and every day.

Dear Mary Ellen,

I'm late again, what can I do,
I am a stinker, I know it's true!

If I could turn the time around
I'd go back to where your birthday is found.

Since the things I do are not great
I'll have to say, "Happy birthday, late!"

So here's to you, a wonderful friend
May your happy days never end.

Let's Help the Work Along!

Have you heard the Prophet say
Study the scriptures every day?
If you do, prepared you'll be
For your mission, you will see.
Let's help the work along!

To love the Lord with all our heart
Let's try His message to impart,
To His children across land and sea,
And truly happy we will be!
Let's help the work along!

To all God's children, now is the time,
From each dollar give a dime,
Every single penny will go,
To help our Father's Kingdom grow.
Let's help the work along!

Let's serve our brother who's in need,
Pay attention and give heed,
To all the things we're sent to do,
To prove our love for God is true.
Let's help the work along!

Our ancestors wait and hope and pray,
Hearts will turn to them one day,
At the temple we'll seal our family,
To last throughout eternity.
Let's help the work along!

Little Children, Do You Know?

Little children, do you know
Heavenly Father loves you so,
He sent to earth His oldeſt son,
To live and die that we may come
Again to dwell with Him above,
In the presence of His pure love.

Little children, have you heard
The scriptures contain Heavenly Father's word?
If we ſtudy them each day
We'll know they are true if we kneel and pray.
They'll help us do our Father's will
Strength obtain and with courage fill.

Little children, make a ſtart!
Love the Lord with all your heart,
Be obedient, kind and true,
Honor Him in all you do.
When your turn at life is paſt,
You may go home to him at laſt.

Respect

Respect and love go hand in hand
Respect is lacking through the land,
Families splitting, road rage and abuse
Signal respect is **NOT** in use.

How can we change this awful plight?
How can we change the wrong to right?
Respecting others is the way to go,
Respect of others helps love flow.

Respecting all God given life.
Respect of husband, Respect of wife,
Showing respect by word and deed.
Respecting children in their need.

Respect of opposing points of view,
Respect is kindness through and through.
Respect is treating others as we would be treated,
Often in the scriptures it has been repeated.

How do we change this selfishness and greed,
To the respect we so desperately need?
Through prayer and service of sisters and brothers,
We gain **self respect**, then we have it for others.

The Power of the Word

The power of the word can make or break a man.
Can build him up, or tear him down,
Can bring both joy and pain.

A word can bring encouragement and hope,
But on the other hand, can dash great aspirations,
Into nothing more than sand.

A word of gentle tenderness, express both love and care,
Though harsh and demanding words,
Bring anger and despair.

A negative word to a child, is oh, so very destructive,
Tearing away their confidence and trust,
Disabling them from being constructive.

When we speak carelessly, or with anger or accusations,
We so easily can crush a tender heart,
misjudging their situations.

Who knows the things that might be achieved,
The greatness or height of a man,
With just a word of encouragement, he will think "I Can!"

We are judged by the words we speak,
Don't pass judgement on what you don't know,
Before speaking remember, You reap that which you sow!

Gossip

Gossip like leaves blows in the wind.

Once it is whispered, it scatters and then,

Like leaves is impossible to gather back in.

Words, once they are spoken can not be unsaid.

Leaving shattered reputations and lives full of dread.

Crushing repentant and innocent lives,

Making change for the better a task of great size.

Which of us is perfect? Who would cast the first stone?

Let's show Christ-like love, or leave them alone.

Gossip and whispers are never a cure,

But make problems larger and innocent victims for sure.

So when you speak of others, don't scatter in the wind,

Leaves of poison you can never gather back in.

The Fragrance of Christmas

The air is filled with the fragrance of Christmas,

Excitement is all around

Wreathes of Holly and Mistletoe

Above the doorways are found.

The glorious tree all shining bright

Sends out to all on this Christmas night

A most lovely Pine perfume.

And through the chill of the frosty air

The aroma goes floating by,

And announces the baking of tasty things

Such as turkey, gingerbread and pie.

There is a fragrance also of sweet breads, cookies and popcorn balls,

And lots of other things

They all remind me of Christmas,

And the joy this holiday brings.

Christmas

This was found in an old, handmade book that belonged to Sharon Hunt. It is unknown whether she is the original author of this poem. A search for this poem returned no results.

Carolers, candles, chimes a ringing,

Holly wreaths with berries clinging,

Reindeer, fairy-fast and tiny,

Icicles all bright and shiny,

Stars and stockings, shoppers streaming

Through the town and tinsel gleaming

Mistletoe in waxen glory,

Angels from the Christmas story,

Santa with his sack to carry...

That spells **CHRISTMAS**
Make it merry!

Grandma & Grandpa

When I was a youngster I loved to go and see,
My grandma and my grandpa who lived not far from me.

Grandma's fridge was always full of yummy things to eat,
Chicken, bread, cake and pie and other tasty treats.

Grandma told me stories of life in days gone by,
She taught me how to tell the time, and how my shoes to tie.

I loved to comb my grandma's hair that she kept piled on her head,
It was so long it nearly touched the floor when she sat upon her bed.

They taught me how to show respect, say thank you and say please,
How to put a smile on even when I skinned my knees.

They taught me always to be honest, truthful and kind,
Never better grandparents could anyone hope to find.

Grandpa liked to tease us children when we came around,
He told us of his "Yay-hoos," who lived hidden under ground.

If you were naughty, you would have to go and stay,
With those big ol' Yay-hoos, and work both night and day.

I helped grandpa in the garden, picking vegetables so young,
Eating as many as I could hold, how sweet upon my tongue.

We sat upon a bench under his big ol' walnut tree,
And as we shelled those big black nuts, he would sing to me.

Grandpa's knees became my horse, they bounced me up and down,
In his pocket he "hid a chick," as he made a chirping sound.

Grandpa always had a song or little game to play.
Visiting my grandparents made, indeed, a happy day!

More Than Just a Mark

Written while serving as a secretary for her LDS ward Relief Society.

A roll card is more than just lines, nice and neat.
It's Relief Society Sisters filling each seat.

Each name in its own alphabetical place,
Stands for a sister of talent and grace,

Let's look at one sister who's name is Shirley,
Her hair is red and not very curly.

Shirley had several talents, but she was real busy,
taking care of her six children sent her into a tizzy.

At the first of the year Shirley came every week,
She came open minded, the Lord's teachings to seek.

Then one week she was sick, no one gave her a call.
The sisters, it seemed, hardly noticed at all.

They had meant to phone or send her a card,
But then, they were busy and thought it too hard—

To bother with extras for just one sister,
So Shirley went on thinking no one had missed her.

Each Sunday came and went, day after day,
And Shirley decided at home it was easier to stay.

Soon sister Shirley was hardly ever there,
And, sadly enough, no one seemed to care.

By the end of the year, Shirley's name was gone,
Off of the roll card, for she had moved on.

But it's not just a mark that is gone from the roll,
It's a name and a face and an eternal soul.

The key to the 99 is the "ONE."

Doby Plays Hookey

Doby was a little boy,
Who thought he hated school,
He decided that he would not go,
He'd imitate a mule.

When his mama came to wake him,
Early Monday morn,
She said, "Hurry and get dressed,
Your breakfast's almost on."

But Doby played possum,
He covered up his head,
He curled in a little lump
At the bottom of his bed.

Again his mama called him,
She wore a little frown,
"You didn't get up at all," she said,
"You're in there upside down!"

"Come on my boy, get up right now,
Or late you're going to be,"
But Doby held the covers tight,
As quiet as a flea.

"Are you ill?" cried his mom,
"I'm worried and distraught!
I'll run and call the doctor,
Perhaps you need a shot!"

Doby heard her footsteps
As she hurried down the hall
He'd better get away real fast,
While his mama made the call!

He jumped from bed into his clothes,
As fast as he could go,
Then out the open window,
To the balcony below.

I do not like to go to school,
I will not go today,
There is nothing worse than spelling words,
It's much more fun to play!

He climbed from the balcony
Into the apple tree,
He started down—but whoops he slipped,
He fell out on his knee.

Poor foolish Doby,
He bumped and scraped his head,
He broke his leg and sprained his arm,
Now he HAS to stay in bed.

Now Doby feels sorry
that he cannot go to school,
He's missing all the parties
And he's under doctor's rule.

His friends come to visit him,
They bring his school assignments
Then they run outside to play,
Leaving him to his confinement.

The Lost Crown

In the land of Let's Pretend
Not so Long ago,
Lived a little fairy girl
by the name of Zo.

Her father was the fairy king,
Her mother was the queen,
They ruled that magic kingdom
The best you've ever seen.

Zo was a happy fairy child,
Most of the time you see
But came a day when she felt bad
She was sad as she could be.

She had a serious problem
Her parents she dared not tell—
For she took her father's crown to play,
And dropped it down the well.

Her father could not do his work
Without his crown you see—
The fairy king must have his crown,
or magic he will not be.

"Courage dear, we'll find it yet,
  You'll see," the queen did say,
"We'll ask our little Zo to help,
  I'll call her now from play."

"Little Zo," her mother said,
"We've lost your father's crown
  We both must help him search for it,
  For he is very down."

Zo did as her mother asked her,
She looked both far and wide,
But she really knew right where it was
She felt so dark inside!

How could she tell her father,
or her mother dear?
What a naughty fairy she had been,
She cried a great big tear.

How could her father love her
When the tale she was to tell
Of how she played with his golden crown
And dropped it down the well?

Everything she thought that day
Was oh, so sad and blue
She cried and how she tried
To think of what to do.

Her little wings began to droop
Her eyes began to swell
How could she hurt her father
And such a story tell?

He'd always loved her dearly
And thought she'd do no wrong
She was his greatest pride and joy
He sang of her in song.

She sat right down against the well
When a big green frog hopped by.
"Why little fairy," he croaked at her,
"What makes you sit and cry?"

"I played with my father's crown
And dropped it down the well
Now he's searching everywhere
And I'm too scared to tell."

"Oh foolish little fairy child,"
 The big green frog did say,
"Go and tell your parents,
 Tell them right away.

"Help your father get his crown,
 Make your mother smile,
 You'll find that telling truth is best,
 Tell it all the while."

 Little Zo jumped right up,
"Thank you my friend, I'll tell!"
 She went at once and told the king
 his crown was in the well.

When Zo had told her father
About her mistake, you see
He put his arms around her,
And set her on his knee.

My darling little daughter,
I am so proud to tell,
You've made me very happy,
though my crown is in the well.

Together, they got a big long hook
And reached down in the well,
They hooked the crown and pulled it out
From the place where it fell.

And now it's time, her father said
For all of us to go,
Out in the woods to the fairy ring
And have a magic show.

To You Dear!

Father's Day, June 15, 2008

You are the love of my life,
You are my strength and my foundation,
I look to you in all I do,
You are my inspiration!

You have always been there in my need
to listen and console,
Or help me see the straight of things,
Or lift in times of woe.

Thank you darling, most of all
for all your love and care,
For your concern and effort,
For the wonderful man you are!

A Valentine

You don't like being sentimental
You aren't much for a lot of fuss
So I'll cut the flowery speeches
And keep this short, no fuss!

The message is stated simply
It's ok for the world to view,
The message is simply this my dear,
I REALLY DO LOVE YOU!

HAPPY VALENTINES DAY!

True Love

To Jay, 2008

In these times of trouble with little peace of
mind,
Marriages are breaking up, true love is hard to
find.
Maybe we don't agree on all the things we do,
But you are very caring, I'm so lucky to have
you!
I can't say that we are wealthy, but I know that
you are true,
You have worked so hard for the children and me.
I truly do LOVE you!!!
For fifty + years you've loved me, what more
could you do?
You have laughed with me, and cried with me,
I'm so blessed that I have you!!!

I'm So Lucky I Have You

Written about 1988. The last verse was found separately from the rest of the poem, among Sharon Hunt's papers. It has been included here for completeness.

In these times of trouble
With little peace of mind,
Marriages are breaking up,
True love is hard to find!
I'm so lucky I've got you!

Maybe we don't agree
On all the things we do,
No matter what,
I know I'm loved!
I'm so lucky I've got you!

I can't say that you're wealthy,
But I know that you are true!
You work so hard
For the kids and me;
I'm so lucky I've got you!

For thirty years you've loved me,
What more could you do?
You've laughed with me
And cried with me;
I'm so lucky I've got you!

You mean the world to me, sweetheart,
Though I am slow to be
The kind of wife that you deserve
You are so good to me!
I'm so lucky I've got you!

God's Handi-Work

Have you seen the early dawn?
Did you look toward the East,
Awed by glowing sunrise
With its wondrous visual feast?

Have you seen the snowy mountain peaks
Caressed by golden sun,
Or the fluffy clouds go floating by
Like ships on their daily run?

This is God's handi-work!

Did you ever see the miles and miles
Of golden rippling grain,
Flowing in the breezes
Of the gently rolling plains?

Have you looked upon the desert
So vast and very still,
The hues and colors changing
Beyond an artist's skill?

This is God's handi-work!

Have you ever fished from a mountain stream,
Or tramped a wooded shore,
Watched the rising of the tide,
And heard the ocean roar?

Late in the evening,
Have you looked toward the West,
And seen the fiery brilliance
Drop beneath the mountain crest?

This is God's handi-work!

And you my friend!
Yes! You and I,
And that little child passing by.
The beasts and birds and things that crawl.

This is <u>all</u> God's handi-work!

A True Friend (Version 1)

You can always depend on a true friend,
They are there with a listening ear,
When you are unwise,
Or grow three times in size,
They are there to support and to cheer,

When you have a true friend you're not lonely,
There is someone with which you can share,
Through good times and bad,
When you think you've been had,
Just reach out and they will be there.

If you are blessed to have found such a friend,
They are worth more than diamonds or gold,
Cherish your friend and then be one,
For true friendship it's found is two-fold.

A True Friend (Version 2)

You can depend on a true friend,
They'll give you a listening ear,
And never betray your confidence,
They are trustworthy, loyal and fair.

If you have a true friend you're not lonely,
When you need them they'll be there,
Helping you through your worst problems,
You know that they truly do care.

If you want a true friend in this world,
The thing that you really must do,
Is be a true friend to others,
And that friendship will come back to you!

The Iverson Family Song

To the tune of "Little Brown Jug."

Once a long, long time ago,
Victor fell in love with Leoma, you know—
She loved him too, and so you see—
They married and started a family.

Oh, ho, ho, it's great to be a member of this family!

The kids grew up and married too.
And that will account for me and you.
We love to get together every year,
It brings us joy and lots of cheer.

Oh, ho, ho, it's great to be a member of this family!

As the years roll by, you can see,
We're building us a family tree
So that one day we can be
A complete and joyous family.

Oh, ho, ho, you and me, we are a happy family!

For our ancestors who have gone,
Our family now must carry on,
Work in the temples while we may,
And ready ourselves for that wondrous day.

Ho, ho, ho, you and me, must live our lives righteously.
Ho, ho, ho, you and me, sealed eternally we can be!

My Country

If I was a poet
As great as I could be,
I'd have a hard time telling
What my country means to me.

The vision of Ol' Glory
Waving oh so high,
Every time I look at it
It makes me want to cry.

When I hear the anthem,
Its beauty does abound,
The chills run up my spine,
My heart begins to pound.

When I see the beauty of this land,
Summer, winter, spring or fall,
I thank the Lord that I was born,
In this choicest land of all.

Cole

Love always, Grandma

So tiny! Yet in such a hurry,
To enter into mortal life,
You couldn't wait, you had to come,
To this world so full of strife.

You gave life a valiant effort,
You taught us more of faith and love,
But it seems that you were needed,
By our Father up above.

So tiny and oh so special,
You didn't need to stay,
So when Heavenly Father called you home
You gladly went away.

We miss you oh so sorely,
Our darling little boy,
Though our thoughts of you are bittersweet
Our hearts are full of joy—

For our knowledge that you have a mission,
As important as can be
Helping to join your family together
For all Eternity.

And we know that you'll be waiting with Jesus,
Your arms opened wide,
To greet each of us as we leave this world,
And come to the other side.

So I'm writing to you this message,
May the Angels make it clear,
I love you more than words can say,
And I look forward to seeing you there!

And if the Father is willing,
I pray that He might just agree,
To allow your presence at special times,
To come and commune here with me.

To Our Little Tristan Rose

To our lovely little Tristan Rose,
Your life was elusive as a beautiful rainbow,
you touched us deeply,
Though your stay was brief as a butterfly—
flitting from flower to flower.
God sent you to us to touch our lives
With a ray of sunshine,
To give us faith and hope.
But, He took you back again
To keep you from the stains of this
Sin filled world.
You were too good, too perfect,
Like a rose in God's garden.
He took you unto Himself to keep your
Lovely petals from being crushed and damaged.

Please God, help us to live so one day
We might join her,
To live forever in thy presence,
To love her and hold her in our arms,
To see her smile and hear her laugh.
Thank you God for sharing with us
Such a sweet and precious flower from thy garden.

Summer Is Gone Again

Last night old Jack Frost
Came sneaking into town
Covering every tree and bush
With a brown and golden gown.

I awoke feeling chilly,
I pulled the covers tight,
I wanted to stay in my warm bed;
Jack Frost was here last night.

The north breeze was whistling
Outside my window pane;
Sighing out the message clear,
That summer is gone again!

The falling leaves were dancing,
Whirling round and round,
Settling down in colored piles,
Upon the frosty ground.

Love in the Old Porch Swing

Swinging slightly on the old porch swing, where many years ago
He asked his love to share his life, just what they did not know.
"Oh yes, oh yes, you know I will," she had said through a teary smile,
I'll walk beside you as you go through life, be it few or many a mile.

Wedding bells rang for the happy pair, together their life had begun,
The first two years were theirs alone, they shared the work and the fun.
The third year brought an additional gift, a cherished baby boy.
How sweet the months that followed, he filled their home with joy.

As the years of life sped forward, they had their ups and downs.
Another son and daughter filled their home with happy sounds.
Though work was hard and money scarce, their life was filled with love,
They worked and played together, and trusted in God above.

The growing years were hectic filled with school, friends and home.
One after another the children grew, and too soon left their parents alone.
They had never been rich (with money), but they never knew,
Money was not the important thing, but God and love so true.

Soon the children were returning with little ones in tow,
With hugs and kisses for Grams and Gramps, the love continued to grow.
Now sitting side by side on the old porch swing where their love began,
They watch the sun as it slowly sinks, as he holds her wrinkled hand.

Royal Birth

I am a Child of Royal Birth
A Child of Heavenly parents
I have been sent to live on Earth
And prove myself to Him.

I have a mission here to fill
To learn and grow and do his will
To serve and to love my fellow man,
As Christ has done for me.

If I start each day by kneeling in prayer
To plead with my Father for His loving care,
I put Him first in all I do.
He'll be with me it's true.

When we go to God's house and do our share,
We'll feel His Spirit and know He's near.

A Step Beyond

Time is etched
Upon her brow,
Ninety plus years
of loving,
Caring,
Toil,
Laughter,
Tears.

Her radiant hair,
Once like new copper,
Has turned
To silver.
Her shoulders,
Are now bent,
From carrying her burden
With courage,
and honor.

Her dim eyes,
Still alert
Look toward tomorrow,
When she
Will step beyond
The curtain of mortality.

She's Gone

Oh that Deep and Empty loneliness
As vast as outer space
The crying out within me
Just once more to see her face.

If only I could turn the clock
around to yesterday
I'd spend my time with her much more
I'd be less cross than e'er before.

Her clothes hang still, upon the rack
Her books behind the door,
The room's the same—yet it has changed,
There's no warmth, no more.

Grandma Sharon's Last Poem

by Brooke Ouzts

Brooke Ouzts, Sharon Hunt's granddaughter, wrote this poem shortly after her grandmother died. Brooke claims to have never successfully completed a poem of her own and that these words came into her mind without any work at all. Brooke feels that this poem is her grandmother's work and titled it as such. Brooke wrote down the verses as they came to her.

When I pass through the veil,
Oh, how wonderful it will be!
I'll see my friends and family
and kiss them tenderly.

Jesus Christ will be there, too,
and say a job well done!
Then take me in his arms
to keep me safe from harm.

I will miss my dear sweet husband,
and children oh so sweet.
But life is a challenge,
we all were eager to meet.

So, I will wait in Heaven,
resting at Jesus' feet.
I will keep watch over
still loving and protecting thee.

48

To Grandpa and Grandma McCain

Grandpa and Grandma, here's to you!
Two of the greatest people I ever knew,
all the sacrifices you made; many untold,
mean to me much more than gold.

Thanks to you for blessings I enjoy today,
It is something I can never repay:
The best that I can offer you,
Is living the Gospel my whole life through.

Also I offer you my love,
And prayers to Father up above,
That when e'er my life is through
I may come and dwell with you.

Index of Titles

www.ingramcontent.com/pod-product-compliance
Lightning Source LLC
Chambersburg PA
CBHW020608030426
42337CB00013B/1265